APPREHENDED
THE PROTOCOL OF PURSUING YOUR PURPOSE

by
Dr. Rick Kendall

Foreward by Dr. Myles Munroe

EMBASSY
PUBLISHING

APPREHENDED

Published by:
Embassy Publishing
P.O. Box 6003
Fort Worth, TX 76115
email: embassypublish@aol.com
Phone: (817) 213-7767
ISBN: 978-0-9830311-5-4

TABLE OF CONTENTS

ENDORSEMENTS

The value of this book is that it compiles under one cover, the process of living a purposed life rather than a hit and miss existence. It will bring the reader to a place of victorious living, with balance and direction in your everyday life. I recommend this work to anyone with a sincere desire to experience life in a meaningful way and to advance God's kingdom here in the earth.

Dr. Gerard Khourie, Pastor of Christ Family International church, Port St Lucie, Florida

Many of us are taking experimental journeys into life without a proper defined purpose. We often find ourselves lost in the jungles of uncertainties and disillusionments that frustrate our existence. Living a life of routine mundane predictabilities can have us going around in circles, draining our energies and making life boring. This heavenly manuscript that God has inscribed into the heart of Dr. Rick Kendall is full of instructions, experiences and protocol that will point us into the direction of our destination. Sometimes all we have to do is stop and ask for direction. Let us stop today from tired living and allow heaven to speak to us through the pen of Dr. Rick Kendall. Let the petals of each page in this book change our lives to purposeful living as we are apprehended by heaven's protocol for effective kingdom living on earth. Thank you Dr. Kendall for listening to the voice of God and releasing his instruction for us on earth, His Kingdom come and his will be done on earth through Kingdom protocols.

R. Pepe Ramnath, PhD Research Scientist/ Author/ Pastor MCCI, Florida

If you want to learn the "M.O." of God's Kingdom and the wisdom of Kingdom protocol, sit at the feet of Dr. Rick Kendall and absorb the principles of this book! It will make all the difference in your walk with the Lord!

Mary Ganster, Operation Safety 91

Every once and a while, someone steps onto the stage of life, that gives meaning to all of us. Dr. Kendall is one of those unique people. He is a man with a purpose and mission, not from himself but from the throne room of God, an apostle for this day and age. When he talks about The Way and not "a" way to getting where God wants His Kingdom people, it is relevant to the principles that God established. "Transition to His Call" or protocol explains from a practical point of view these standards that God has set forth. I have said for the past 20 years, "God is getting us ready, for what He already has ready for us." Dr. Kendall has captured the spirit of this in this book. NOW is the time to move forward in the Body of Christ to obtain what God has set forth for us, and not keep living below the standard. This book makes apprehending a possible concept, which has always been God's plan for us to take back our Dominion through Jesus, and the power of the Holy Spirit.

Dr. Jerry Wilkes, Faith Church, Hobe Sound, Florida

We are privileged to live during an intersection in time, when God is using certain of his servants to bring his people into a better understanding of the message that Jesus taught, the Kingdom of God, and our role in it . In Apprehended, Dr. Rick Kendall, takes you on a journey in practically defining, the progressive process, pursuit, and orderly implementation of one's purpose as it relates to destiny in the Kingdom of God. As you immerse yourself in the pages of this book you will be gripped by thought provoking revelation and truth communicated by a seasoned man of God. This enlightening book will encourage you to take a personal assessment of your purpose, as well as give you a better understanding of the protocol and continuum of apprehension. This book is a must read for those who desire to gain insight, and understanding of the definitive process of embracing God's Kingdom purpose and assignment for their life.

Dr. Darrell Wilson, Acts Church Ministries International, Fort Worth, Texas

The book "Apprehended" by Dr. Rick Kendall is a beautiful and eye opening revelation of Kingdom living. I wholeheartedly recommend this book for all believers looking and wondering, "Where do I fit in God's wonderful plan?" These rules of Kingdom protocols will transform us -not only to become better citizens of the Kingdom, but into Ambassadors who will impact all areas of the world with the Kingdom of God.

Dr. David Donnally, Evangelical Bible Chapel and Seminary, Lake Worth, Florida

IV APPREHENDED

DEDICATION

The primary dedication of this book is to Liz, my wife of 39 years. She constantly stretches my capacity to be more of what God has purposed me to be, and she challenges me to expect God to do greater things as we walk through the stages of God's protocol development together. She has given me three outstanding children: Ricky, Jonathan, and Victoria, to whom I also dedicate this book. They amaze me as they navigate through their own discoveries of God's purpose that will far excel anything I have ever done. In addition, I want to dedicate this book to my Dad and Mom, Richard and Dorothy Kendall, who founded me in the absolutes of character and integrity. Finally, this book is dedicated to Dr. Myles Munroe who continues to invest himself freely into the countless scores of spiritual sons and daughters all over the world to birth the rediscovery of the Kingdom of God in multiple generations to come.

VI   APPREHENDED

SPECIAL THANKS

There are so many in my circle of family and friends that I could give mention of special thanks, but I will name just a few here. Thank you to my friend and pastor Gerard Khourie who encourages me continually. Thanks to Dr. Paula Price who's deeply profound insights and books inspired me to write. Thank you to Jim Collins who spent countless hours helping me to edit this book to bring expression into clarity. Finally special thanks to those three financial investors who believed this first book needed to be published.

VIII APPREHENDED

FOREWORD:

This erudite, eloquent, and immensely thought-provoking work gets to the heart of the deepest passions and aspirations of the human heart to achieve success in life. "Apprehended" is indispensable reading for anyone who wants to live life above the norm. This is a profound authoritative work which spans the wisdom of the ages and yet breaks new ground in its approach and will possibly become a classic in this and the next generation.

This exceptional work by Rick Kendall is one of the most profound, practical, principle-centered approaches to this subject of Protocol I have read in a long time. The author's approach to this timely issue brings a fresh breath of air that captivates the heart, engages the mind and inspires the spirit of the reader. The author's ability to leap over complicated theological and metaphysical jargon and reduce complex theories to simple practical principles that the least among us can understand is amazing.

This work will challenge the intellectual while embracing the laymen as it dismantles the mysterious of the soul search of mankind and delivers the profound in simplicity. Rick's fresh approach to the concept of Protocol awakens in the reader the untapped inhibiters that retard our personal development and his antidotes empower us to rise above these self-defeating, self-limiting factors to a life of exploits in spiritual and mental advancement.

The author also integrates into each chapter the time-tested precepts giving each principle a practical application to life making the entire process people-friendly. Every sentence of this book is pregnant with wisdom and I enjoyed the mind-expanding experience of this exciting book. I admonish you to plunge into this ocean of knowledge and watch your life change for the better. Follow the protocol in the book and see your life emerge to his true greatness.

Dr. Myles Munroe
BFM International
ITWLA
Nassau Bahamas

INTRODUCTION

Driving through the mountains, Liz and I were traveling to a speaking engagement. We had a map unfurled trying to interpret the directions because this was the first time we had been in that particular region of the country. We had great excitement about where we were going, but the further we went the further our destination seemed out of reach. As our journey took us higher into the mountains we stopped to ask directions at an antique gas station where a very old man sat with a grin on his face. I rolled down my window, told the man the name of the town we needed to get to and asked, "How do we get there from here?" He sat forward and declared, "You can't get there from here!"

There are many people feeling that way spiritually. They have destiny, but have taken so many faulty turns that they feel they can not get to where they are going from where they are. The conclusion many draw is that they might as well stop short of their dreams and set up camp just outside of their potential. In Numbers chapter 14, we find the account of the Israelites and their frustration in the wilderness as they kept going around the same mountain. This was completely unnecessary because they were within eyeshot of the promise land. They assumed they could not get there because of the giant roadblocks, and as a result, camped outside of their promised land for 40 years.

The truth is that God ordained our purpose and destiny before we were even formed in our mother's womb. God knew all the obstacles we would face, so the GOOD NEWS is you **can** get "there" from here, but it will take obedience to the steps that are ORDERED by the Lord. This journey will indeed involve a daily transformation of our mindsets because God is not only preparing our places, but He is preparing us for those places as we are processed with each ordered step. The gas station attendant was really saying that if I tried to get "there" by forging ahead in my current direction, it would result in driving off the side of the mountain, but if I wanted to get "there" alive I would need to go back down the mountain and make a right turn at the bridge. He was giving me directions to process my progress. Progress with no process is nothing more than an exercise in futility. Actually, the gas station attendant was issuing protocol that would open access into my destination so that I could get "there" from here.

Sitting around in the wilderness condemning ourselves for missing a road sign will not get us any where, and becoming egotistical to prove our "short cuts" were right will result in a drive off the side of a cliff. My prayer is that this book will become a revelation of Kingdom protocol to process your purpose through to manifested promises set by God.

PREFACE

Our lives must have a sense of significance and destiny that ignite our passion. A journey without purpose is a stroll in circles, and routine without progress is a rut that used to be a path but lost sight of a destination. Too many are just "existing" through life allowing circumstances to define them while becoming the sum total of experiences they face. God has ordained specific purpose into every human being before they were even born and planted deep within them the seed of promise with the potential to discover it. The moment we discover the original blueprint of our lives through Jesus Christ, who is the revealed Word of God, we are free from the bondage of false identity and made alive to discover who we really are in the destiny God has set for us. This revelation on purpose apprehends us in every fiber of our being. The apostle Paul expressed it this way, "Not as though I had already attained, either were already perfect: but I follow after, if that I may apprehend that for which I also am apprehended of Christ Jesus…(and) I PRESS (literally protocol) toward the mark for the prize of the high calling of God in Christ Jesus" (Philippians 3:12, 14). Even though God has already predestined the road for our destiny it does not mean we will automatically get there. The prize we are pressing toward is not in achievements along the way or the applause and recognition of people, but the prize is in Christ Jesus, the very blueprint of God who holds the pattern of who we were born to be. Camping out at a high point (or low point) of our lives, thinking that we have "arrived" to a full definition of who we are, will stunt our growth and cause us to "come short" of the bigger picture. I have personally been walking with the Lord for over 40 years now and I feel I have only scratched the surface of discovering who He is and who I am becoming. When we become alive to God's purpose, a fire of passion is ignited to serve Him completely. This begins the process of PRESSING to apprehend what has apprehended us. We are in love with God, not just because of what He gives us or because He got us out of hell (although we are certainly thankful for that), but because God is our very reason for living. Our life is no longer going backwards through debts from the past, but launching ahead in the promise of tomorrow in our today through cultivating a purposed lifestyle.

You are not an accident. Your life has significance even when you cannot feel it. God's passion is working His plan deep in the belly of who you are. Your life is not left to the dictates of life's ups and downs, but even in difficult places, God has set a sure course ahead that actually turns things around for good to them who are the CALLED according to His purpose. God sees the end from the beginning and will fulfill all He apprehended us to be and accomplish all He called us to do. This is sealed with covenant promise and it is absolute.

Chapter 1
Defining the Process
of Kingdom Protocol

Philippians 3:12 not only speaks of Paul's passion to apprehend the purpose and destiny that apprehended his total being, but in verse 14 he outlines a process of pressing (or protocol) to get him from where he is to where God has already set him to arrive. The mark is the goal that identifies the prize set in the high calling of God in Christ Jesus. We will discover that there are no shortcuts in the cultivation of destination in God's Kingdom.

When some think of protocol they may think of "ceremonial etiquettes" or unnecessary Bureaucracy, but God's protocol is actually a major factor in the cultivating of purpose. You can have sound doctrine, but without the PROTOCOL to carry it forth it will not work. There is protocol in every facet of our lives.

While the word protocol is not used in the scriptures, we find it throughout the Bible in the form of the word "order." A Greek word for **ORDER** is "taxis," which means to ordain, give rank, position, authority, and succession. (See Hebrews 5:10; 6:20; 7:17-21.) In technology, protocol is further defined as a set of rules to communicate fully as it is the process of routing data exchange, interchange, and interconnection. In international diplomatic circles protocol is a go between, and it involves customs and regulations for intercultural exchange and negotiation. The word "protocol" also comes from two other Greek words, which mean "first" and "glue." Therefore, protocol is involved in how we interact and inter-connect with one another. Global protocol can be further summed up as:

1. **Code of Conduct:** productive behavior of an individual or organization.
2. **Functional Agreement**: operations between authorities and procedures.
3. **Ethics and Etiquette:** observed between governments, ambassadors, diplomats, heads of corporate organizations, ministries, and nations.
4. **A globally recognized standard:** of relational collaboration and interconnectivity between functionally accountable relationships.

Although some would like to skip these steps and get on with seizing their destiny now, doing that would result in driving off the side of a spiritual cliff and aborting the potential of apprehending. **Like the piece of a PUZZLE, protocol is about knowing WHERE we fit and HOW we fit together.** It includes the process of cultivating a citizenship who interact in combined yet individual destiny. As the old song says, "No man is an island." The Word of God confirms this when it says that we are a fitly framed citizenship. (See Ephesians 2:19-22.)

There are several words within the word protocol. "Pro" means to see the end result at the beginning. "Protos" is order. "Protocollon" is defined as a process through ("colon").

"Prokopto" means to advance. God has called each one of us to prophetic purpose, and protocol is the processing order God has set to a resulting destination before we even start. PROTOCOL could be summed up as a **PRO-through to His CALL.**

Note: PROTOCOL will produce **transformation, transition, and transfer**. To omit any aspect of protocol stalls progress in our lives causing a rut of our own doing. Repenting of shortcuts and yielding ourselves to God's principles will get us on the road of progress again. Protocol does not depend on a feeling, a whim, or ideal circumstances. Protocol depends only on the plan of God that overcomes all obstacles.

A WORD about PROTOCOL in REVERSE: When Adam, the original man, disobeyed God and sinned, he reversed the protocol of God's process in the earth and things began moving backwards into perversion. Mankind became "apprehended," but apprehended in bondage to a corrupted state of being. A curse is basically a blessing in reverse. When Adam sinned against God's process of dominion, he became disconnected from God. The Kingdom was lost and inaccessible to man who was supposed be God's agent of set order.

The PROCESS of PROTOCOL RESTORED: The second Adam, Jesus, came and reversed the curse by taking our transgressions on Himself, thus restoring us to God. He reconnected us to the original cultivation process of purpose. We are now called the RIGHTEOUSNESS of God in Christ. Righteousness is not just a religious term; it means to be JUSTIFIED (made right with God). None of the protocol of purpose will work if we do not WALK in righteousness. Knowing that we are in right standing with God allows us to become all

God says we already are – the righteousness of God in Christ. That is why it is called a WALK (with steps). It does not mean we will not miss the mark at times or that we are already fully perfected; it means that our LIFE is committed and consecrated to the purpose of God and that we are yielded to Him as our reason for living. Righteousness is not just an outward show because what good is it if the outside of a cup appears clean, but the inside is filthy.

Righteousness is also more than adhering to rules. Righteousness is the transformational protocol of discovery and recovering of who we really are that peels off any false identity. 2 Corinthians 5:17 says, "Therefore if any man be in Christ, he is a new creature (creation): old things are passed away, behold, all things are become (developing) new." Verse 18 goes on to say, "And (now) all things are of God, who hath reconciled us to himself by Jesus Christ, and hath given to us the ministry of reconciliation." In other words, now we are involved in reconciling people to what God restored back to us. We are not casual observers, but instead we are becoming better representatives of God's Kingdom. Verse 20 and 21 go on to say, "Now then we are ambassadors for Christ, as though God did beseech you by us (or as though the King Himself were standing here in front of you): we pray you in Christ's stead, be reconciled to God. For he hath made him to be sin for us, who knew no sin; that we might be made the righteousness of God in him."

This is the protocol of God's government to achieve reconciliation to our place as citizens of His dominion. We are called Ambassadors because we are sent forth by God's Kingdom into the foreign soil of a corrupted world system where we are commissioned to establish embassies (outposts of

God's authority) set to activate and equip more ambassadors. Ambassadors are a "passage-through-doors" as they function in the protocol of the King they represent. These representatives move through the infiltration of influence into the world with the fire of renovation that brings down the strongholds of enemy principalities that once prevented our original purpose.

In Matthew 16:16-18, a disciple named Peter had a revelation of Jesus the Christ and His purpose of restoring God's plan. Jesus responded to Peter this way, "Flesh and blood (or conventional thinking) didn't give you this revelation, but you got it from My Father in heaven, so I'm declaring you to be a part of this Rock solid foundation, and upon this revelation of restored Kingdom connection I will build My church (embassy), and as a result, the gates of hell shall not prevail against it."

The eternal Kingdom of God, through Jesus Christ, re-opened mankind to his God ordained mandates that were lost through Adam's acceptance of an inversion of a couple of words twisted by the devil. Jesus, who is the Word and became a man, refused the temptation of twisted words by the enemy and defeated the devil by declaring the proper protocol of the Word emerging in the power of God's Spirit. That is how important the protocol of God is even in something as seemingly small as misplacing a couple of words that changes the proper meaning of a process. Kingdom protocol functions not to be a legalistic set of rules to restrain us into mediocrity, but instead to propel us into purpose. Kingdom protocol is a legal (and governmentally Kingdom backed) process to FREE us from stumbling into deceptive shortcuts of the enemy so that we can reach our destination with accuracy.

A REVIEW OF PRINCIPLES IN CHAPTER ONE

1. There is protocol in every facet of our lives that is attached to set purpose.

2. While the word protocol is not used in the scriptures, we find it throughout the Bible in the form of the word "order."

3. PROTOCOL could be summed up as **PRO-through to His CALL.**

4. The results of PROTOCOL are to **transform, transition, and transfer.**

5. When the original man Adam disobeyed God and sinned, he reversed the protocol of God's process in the earth.

6. Jesus, the second Adam, came to the earth and reconnected us to the cultivation process of protocol.

7. We are called Ambassadors because we are sent into the foreign soil of a corrupted world system to activate the protocol of Kingdom restoration.

CHAPTER TWO
APPREHENDING THE WAY AND PATH OF PROTOCOL

Protocol cannot move or progress without the grounds to do it. Many have been apprehended with passion about the discovery of purpose, but stuck in the rut of not knowing how to go forward. Throughout Scripture, God called his pioneers to establish GROUND after a long journey in the wilderness God revealed the promise land to Moses. What made it the promise land was not the "land," but the promise attached to it. The promise itself proclaimed what it would be before it was manifested to the physical eye. Even though the land was full of milk and honey, most could only see the primitive jungle and giant obstructions. In Joshua 1:3, Moses told Joshua and the people of Israel: "Every place that the sole of your foot shall TREAD upon, that have I given unto you as I said unto Moses." Most of the time the ground ahead appears undeveloped and overgrown with weeds, but the path has already been set before the foundation of the world.

Taking ground does not always mean seizing existing real estate in its current form. Jericho was a fully developed functional city, but it could not be inhabited by God's people due to corruption; it first had to be brought down flat. Obedience to the protocol of God's command is vital in insuring that we progress into how God is cultivating that ground.

Every piece of ground has the WAY and the PATH God has ordained. Please note: It is not just "a way" but THE WAY. Wrong perceptions and conventional thinking can cause us to miss strategic avenues by substituting self-made roads. God makes a way where none seemed to be. Isaiah 43:16 says that God makes a way in the sea and a path in the mighty waters. This is certainly not a conventional path as most would look for (like a solid concrete sidewalk), nor is it about walking in the way things appear now. God's WAY and PATH were set BEFORE the sea and waters were displaced by the sin of mankind. In other words, God is setting us in creative protocol to OPEN His paths again no matter how things appear today. The Kingdom course we are on is not about today; it is about restoring what was and is to come by activating prophetic destiny into our TODAY. You might say we are going back to the future.

Isaiah 43 goes on to say in verse 19: "Behold I do a new thing; now shall you not know it? I will even make a way in the wilderness, and rivers in the desert." Conventional thinking waits until it gets out of the desert to find a way, but God does a new thing that opens His WAY, revealing His PATH right in the middle of what seemed impossible. When rivers spring forth IN a desert it ceases to be a desert. In seemingly "dry" places, there is a river of God's innovation getting ready to explode. Remember, things are not always as they appear, and paradigms can change quickly to make way for God's ordained purpose. Psalm 25:4 says: "Show me Your ways, O Lord, teach me Your path!"

The WAY is defined as an opening. It is much more than a "loophole" or "escape" to get out of trouble; it is an innovative pattern, blueprint, and process that gets us into fulfilling our purpose. Jesus didn't just say He "knows the way," but He declared "I am the way," full of the TRUTH (or path) that opens the protocol (process) of LIFE (John 14:6). The WAY manifested became revealed innovation reopening paths that had become overgrown with the weeds of man's corruption.

A PATH is defined as a route with specific direction with specific points of reference and direction along the WAY. The path of purpose does not always appear fully paved and cannot always be seen with the physical eye, but as we shared, it often leads over waters and even though it has been blueprinted in eternity, we can only see it through the spiritual eye of vision.

The rediscovery of these paths is the focus Jesus was talking about in Luke 9:62. Jesus said: "No man, having put his hand to the plow, and looking back, is fit for the kingdom of God." Often people refer to this verse as meaning "to stick to a task." The principle Jesus was sharing had more to it than a "works" message, because after all, the plow is doing most of the work. He was sharing a VISIONARY MESSAGE! The purpose of the plow is to OPEN UP the greater prophetic purpose of ground that was there (but not yet revealed), and simultaneously start the CULTIVATION of Kingdom development. A person cannot operate a plow by looking behind them because the function of the plow is focused opening up NEW PATHS and GROUND that will reveal KINGDOM re-entry and manifestation. No one putting their HAND to the PLOW and LOOKING BACK is FIT for Kingdom progress. There is no way to look "cool" or stylish while working a plow because the plow is also working you. Before the plow can cultivate the ground ahead of us, it must cultivate us and our ability to see ahead. This UGLY, AWKWARD tool turns out to be a CUTTING EDGE of VISION as God cultivates us into the discovery of His Kingdom in the earth. No matter how awkward you feel right now, rejoice in this WONDERFUL pioneering mandate!

A Review of Principles in Chapter Two

1. Protocol cannot move or progress without ground.

2. God has ordained His WAY and His PATH for protocol to advance.

3. The **WAY** is defined as a blueprint and process that gets us into fulfilling our purpose.

4. A **PATH** is defined as a route of specific direction with specific points of reference.

5. The purpose of the plow is to OPEN preordained paths that were previously hidden.

Chapter 3
The Protocol of Apprehending Purpose and Passion

These desires that have apprehended us are not just emotional feelings, but instead, we have been "arrested" and held captivated to set purpose. God's PURPOSE for our lives is a continual discovery through process, and as we have discussed, process has specific protocols set by God to move us into our destiny no matter how many obstacles or setbacks we face. Many people make the mistake of assuming they know their purpose fully by identifying it as something they want to do based on where they are in a particular level of growth. Purpose is a continual PROCESS of "being." Purpose first focuses on "why" we are before knowing "what" we are going to do with our lives. Too many people rush the process and get their identity and worth by what they do and do not fully discover who they are. The protocol of purpose goes beyond current status, occupations, ministries, and even successful positions. It is defined as the totality of who you were designed to be by God. While we inhabit a physical earth suit for a space of time, we are eternal beings with a part in an eternal plan.

Your God ordained purpose will continually shape, shift, and transform you into becoming who God says you already are. People who stop embracing the constant discovery of purpose begin to harden into a cynical reflection of the combined hard times they face. If we stop the process of growth we stop living even though we may continue to breath and walk around in a daily routine. The protocol of purpose does not mean we will not face difficulty, but it means our ordained destiny will make a way to get through it.

Many years ago my wife and I lived in a house that was in a downtown area where houses were elevated several feet above the sidewalk. To get up to the house porch from street level you had to climb about ten concrete steps to make it to the top. One day I was facing a particularly difficult time in my ministry. I went out to sit on the porch at the top of the concrete steps to basically feel sorry for myself. While looking down I saw an amazing sight. There, up through all those concrete steps, was a flower that had somehow made it to the top and had found a little crack in the concrete to burst forth and boldly display its glory. Viewing that scene, I quickly decided my current crisis was nothing in comparison to that tender looking flower. If that flower had the determination to persist through all that concrete, thus fulfilling its purpose, then certainly I could overcome my small situation.

Jesus made it clear in John 10:10 that the devil is a very real thief. He has a counterfeit protocol that attempts to extract life out of us by coming to kill our purpose by stealing our dreams so he can destroy our hope. Satan does not mind if we are still alive physically as long as we cease to be alive in purpose. He will do what he can to distract us with some crisis in an attempt to derail our hope, but John 10:10 goes on to say that Jesus has COME to stop the thief, give us back our LIFE, and insure us that we will actually have life more abundantly.

PURPOSE declares the **"who"** and **"why"** we are. The Greek word for **PURPOSE** is *"prothesis"* or the **"pro"** to God's **"thesis"** (literally, His theme, reason, and pattern of our being). Dr. Myles Munroe says: **"Purpose sets our end result at the beginning."** We can run from it, miss it, and even reject it, but God's ordained purpose is absolute, and true peace can only be experienced in life by accepting it. We are **CALLED (eternally), SEALED (royally)**, and **APPOINTED (prophetically)** in **purpose** to **move (by protocol)** through an immovable Kingdom into unshakable destiny.

PASSION is the direct result of purpose. Passion is more than intense affection for someone or something. Passion is the DELIGHT and DESIRE that pours from the belly of who we are. Passion also has distinctive protocol as described in Psalm 37:4, which says: **"Delight** thyself also in the Lord; and He shall give thee the **desires** of thine heart."** If our delight is in the Lord, He will give His PASSION expressed through the PURPOSE of our heart (or inner-man). Your greatest passion reveals clues to your overall purpose. Every person has a passion of some kind, but we need to examine ourselves to make sure our motives are pure and the fire of passion is operating in the protocol of purpose lest it get caught up in an aspect of current involvement and we lose sight of the bigger picture. Passion not centered in God ordained purpose can become corrupted. For example:

1) Passion misdirected is hatred.
2) Passion perverted is lust.
3) Passion self-centered is greed.
4) Passion trapped is distress.
5) Passion misplaced is apathy.

Passion does not drive purpose, but purpose must drive passion. We must also be sure that we do not mistake passion for our purpose. People get so fired up (passionate) about what they are currently "doing" that they often lose sight of the bigger picture of purpose and run off the road to chase accomplishments instead of pursuing the apprehension of a higher prize. Psalm 37:23 states that the STEPS (path) of a GOOD MAN (purposed) are ORDERED (in protocol) by the Lord and he delights (is passionate) in His WAY. The first part of Isaiah 58:14 says: "Then shalt thou **DELIGHT** thyself in the Lord; and I will cause thee to **RIDE UPON** the **HIGH PLACES** of the earth." Without God's protocol our ordained purpose will sit unprocessed. Our passion will have plenty of fuel, but will be trapped motionless. Many who started a good journey have shipwrecked, not in the big decisions, but in the seemingly insignificant side-steps. Ignoring the detailed process of God in small issues can become a huge stumbling block later.

A Review of Principles
in Chapter Three

1. Purpose is the process of first "being," and second, "why" we are before it is about knowing "what" we are going to do with our life.

2. The process of purpose does not mean we will not face difficulty, but it means our ordained destiny will make a way to get through it.

3. The Greek word for **PURPOSE** is *"prothesis"* or the **"pro"** to God's **"thesis."**

4. Passion is the DELIGHT and DESIRE that pours from the belly of purpose.

5. Passion does not drive purpose but purpose must drive passion.

6. Without God's protocol our ordained purpose will sit unprocessed. Our passion will have plenty of fuel, but will be trapped motionless.

CHAPTER 4
PROTOCOL OF APPREHENDING
VISION AND MISSION

VISION is the spiritual eyesight of purpose so we can comprehend what is apprehending us. Vision is the ability to see what God has been saying. Vision is looking further than our eyes can see. A vision is a prophetic look into what we are becoming, where we are headed before we get there, and understanding how we are developing along the way. Vision is not just about having knowledge or intellectual ingenuity. Vision is about being seasoned into the bigger scope of wisdom to know times and seasons.

The subject of "having a vision" is sometimes viewed as a mysterious religious event, or simplified as a set of new ideas and plans. However, like everything else God does in our lives, VISION is a developing process of perception designed to solve the mysteries unfolding before us.

Vision has a protocol within the protocol of developing purpose. God-given vision does not just reveal things as they happen, it shows us what God has already done but is yet to be manifested in our lives. One of the Greek words for vision is "optomai," from which come the words "optometry" and "optical" (having to do with eyesight). The physical eye takes in a series of pictures and information to assess where we are. While there are certainly accounts in Scripture of actual events where God set instantaneous spiritual displays before the eyes of people for immediate action (such as Acts 9:12, Acts 11:5, Acts 16:9), most of the visions (referred to in Scripture) have to do with prophetic insight and revealed direction to be processed over time.

Proverbs 29:18 says; "Where there is no vision the people perish; but he that keeps the law, happy is he." In other words, where there is no "oracle" or clear visionary leadership, people cast off their strength to carry on, but those that will continue processing the law (or principles) they've already received will maintain their stand secure until the next level of progress comes. Having a vision does not mean all details are fully comprehended immediately, but as already stated, a vision is the process of revelation that cultivates us and opens greater understanding of the concepts of God's purpose set in our lives.

Many young men and women of God have shared the frustration that they have not yet "had a vision." While frustration is never fun, it is an indicator that our inner man knows there is deeper truth yet to be discovered, but the mind has not yet grasped it. Often the greater the level of challenge equals the greater the level of revelation that ultimately processes into vision. It is important to remember, however, that the priority is not to "seek" a sign, but to process the principles that keep us stable and sure until the next revelation comes. Vision may not come in the form of angels appearing with harps in the middle of the night, but it might just explode into a series of insights through your passion to discover more of the unsearchable riches of God. When we seek His face and not just His hands we get both.

The Hebrew word for "vision" (in Proverbs 29:18) is "chazah." It means "to gaze upon," "behold," and "to process" a revelation. The problem with some of the "church world" today is that it has become too event driven. There is nothing wrong with events or revivals, but often some have thought a miracle or a one night instant breakthrough would jumpstart a vision. This is not God's protocol. God never starts with a manifestation, but He first begins by activating a move. God's MOVE begins deep underground as a process where vision develops before it is manifested through the soil out into full view where all can see it. Vision is not the ability to gather people around what you are doing, or with buildings you want to construct, but instead, VISION is the reason WHY you are progressing into something. Vision moves into helping people understand their own individual vision that fitly frames them together to know their part corporately.

A **MISSION** is the outgrowth of **VISION**. Mission is not vision, and a mission never produces vision. Many burn out by copying someone else's MISSION and calling it their VISION. Mission is WHAT we do out of the WHY of vision. The current mission is not WHO we are, it is simply a product of who we are.

To think that mission will give us vision to become our purpose is precisely backwards to the protocol God has set forth. Priority in protocol is vital. This is the reason why Jesus made it clear that we must FIRST SEEK the KINGDOM of GOD (where purpose is founded) and HIS RIGHTEOUSNESS (our identity), and all these other THINGS (thoughts, ideas, works) will be added (Matthew 6:33) It is important to note that collective "steps" become a "walk" that sets our "way." We must take heed to the why and how of what we do," lest we miss the mark of purposed potential.

A REVIEW OF PRINCIPLES
IN CHAPTER FOUR

1. **VISION** is the spiritual eyesight of purpose so we can comprehend it.

2. **VISION** has a protocol working within the protocol of developing purpose.

3. The Hebrew word for vision (in Proverbs 29:18) is "chazah," which means "to gaze upon," "behold," and to "process" a revelation.

4. A **MISSION** is the outgrowth of VISION.

5. A **MISSION** never produces VISION.

6. We must FIRST SEEK the KINGDOM of GOD where purpose is founded, and then mission can be produced.

CHAPTER FIVE
THE PROTOCOL OF APPREHENDING OUR PART IN COMMUNITY

We cannot pursue the apprehending of our destiny alone. In fact, God reveals throughout His Word how vital interconnecting (or fitly framing) our destiny with other fellow-citizens is to fulfilling our destiny and how essential it is to cultivating His Kingdom here on this planet. I once heard someone say, "I would have a successful ministry if I didn't have to mess with all these people." I think the person that said that missed the whole point of ministry. Even though that statement sounds ridiculous, there are some who actually feel this way because they assess that their calling in life is only about their own fulfillment.

The day of the superstar leader who puts focus solely on the fame of their name is coming to an end. The problem with superstars is that they are like a "meteor" (independent of a larger planet) that rises fast but burn out quick. A "lone ranger" (so-called) type of leadership often is an opportunist seeking relationship only long enough to advance their agenda. While there are people of integrity who are famous, being famous does not automatically mean they have integrity. Relationships must be a two way street with God's purpose as the motive for every level of interconnecting, because, if not, ulterior motives collide, protocol is disabled, and progress slows. The reason 2

Corinthians 6:14 says not to be unequally yoked together with unbelievers is because the protocol of LIGHT is on a different path than the road of darkness (ignorance). We should reach out to all people, but we MUST choose our friends wisely. The deeper the relationship the more we should examine if it is serving the purpose of God. Leadership carries a great weight of responsibility. If the leadership you are submitted to is a dictatorship or a superstar club, it may be time to seek another company of people. Every Kingdom level of relationships has a particular protocol dynamic of interaction.

For example, a "mentor" and a "protégé" have a unique developmental process. The intent of genuine spiritual fathers (men and women of God) is not to gain permanent students who look like them, but to raise up generations of champions that excel anything they have ever done. These kinds of leaders are not idols, they are heroes to those who have been activated into their Kingdom call.

One of the most powerful definitions of relational protocol found in Ephesians 2:19-22. This portion of scripture declares that we are no longer strangers and foreigners, but fellow citizens with the saints operating in the household of God and built upon the foundation of apostles and prophets, Jesus Christ Himself being the chief corner stone IN WHOM all the building fitly frames together to grow into a holy temple in the Lord, as a habitation of God through the Spirit. We are not islands unto ourselves, but interconnected Kingdom citizens and "living stones" fitly framed together as a household. In the New Testament, we are no longer referred to as a "congregation," but (through Jesus Christ) we are now an interconnected BODY of fitly framed citizens yoked into the headship of our King.

Congregations could only "watch" God move, and although they moved as tribes, they were still individually unable to partake in the holy of holies due to sin separating them from God and each other. Jesus, the first-fruits of God's Kingdom (manifested in flesh on this earth), REDEEMED, RESTORED, and RECONCILED us back into His Father's Kingdom to become extensions of His very Body on the planet. Now, we are no longer disconnected sojourners, but grafted in and assembled members of His headship and governmental branches of Kingdom authority. Hebrews 10:20 refers to the paradigm shift (activated through Christ) as a "new and living WAY." In other words, PROTOCOL shifted into gear.

This Protocol of household operation oils the gears of God's people in **relational, governmental, and operational** function to cultivate a unique community of people with destiny. In fact, 1 Corinthians 12:4-6 refers to these as functions as **gifts, administrations, and operations**. How we interact relationally with individuals, organizations, and nations will determine how far we get in the realization of our purpose. Some may refer to this as "people skills," but it is much more than that. Here are some scriptural examples of **relational protocol** on multiple levels.

1. Philippians 2:3 We must "esteem others higher than ourselves. (general)

2. 1 Timothy 5:1 Rebuke not an elder. (seniority)

3. Ephesians 5:21 Submit to one another in the fear of God. (church)

4. Ephesians 5:25 Husbands love your wives as Christ loved the church. (marriage)

5. 1 Chronicles 16:22 Touch not mine anointed and do my prophets no harm. (authority)

6. Exodus 20:3-17 God's law and the protocols of conduct are not suggestions, but commandments.

The list above contains just a few of the many protocols referring to the engagement and process of relationships on various levels. These connections will determine how far we advance without having to backtrack. We will only go as far as we are willing to properly "fitly frame" with others. Some would like to quickly promote themselves into great titles and positions with no process or transitional development. Jesus, however, made it clear that "he who will be great in the Kingdom learns to serve first." He said this not just as an exercise in humility, but to determine motivation through character building. There are God-given offices and mantles defining function and authority that carry the responsibility of leadership. Submission to God's ordained authority is not about being weak, but it is about the protocol to promotion and diplomatic power.

Before God constructs great accomplishments, He cultivates the character of people. We are redeemed citizens who have become an extension of His very name and nature. We are an embassy of ambassadors representing God, functioning in activated governmental protocol, and SET on a FOUNDATION. We are ESTABLISHED on an unmovable FOUNDATION of apostles and prophets, Jesus Christ Himself being the CHIEF CORNERSTONE. This is not just a "visitation" from God, but we are actually built for the HABITATION of GOD.

The Apostle represents God's architect, the one who sets order and activates components according to the blueprint (or pattern) of God's plan.

The Prophet represents God's visionary contractor who sees and declares the next season or time for construction before it manifests.

Jesus Christ (the Chief Cornerstone) represents the entire blueprint and pattern of God's eternal purpose activating us as lively stones for God to dwell in (1Peter 2:5-9).

The **PURPOSE** and the **VISION** are not in a current stage of building, but they are in the foundation. The FOUNDATION is not just the beginning of construction, but continues to support and develop a PROPHETIC FUTURE a each level. Wisdom will take inventory of what people are building and it will question whether what they are building is still set on the foundation. There are many people wearing themselves out building things for God that He never blueprinted. Some who started building God's design encountered rejection and disappointment, and as a result of allowing this to discourage them, began building weapons and huts to hide in. The foundation of God is crying out to those wounded champions to be delivered and regain their God-given dreams by revisiting the Rock of their purpose.

Most people will take note of how beautiful a house is without noticing the foundation. They tend to think that the foundation was important in the beginning before the house started construction, and now they think there is little need to refer to it. However, in God's economy, the foundation is vital for continuing development EVERYDAY because the prophetic blueprint of PURPOSE and VISION are embedded in it.

The FOUNDATION of God brings accountability, integrity, accuracy, and obedience as requirements to the ongoing building of His household. Anyone foolish enough to think that they can build on their own terms will find themselves on shifting sand when the storms come. The wise know that it is not necessarily how high you can build a thing, it is how firm the foundation is set that determines if that house will stand. There is no other foundation to build on except Jesus Christ, the living blueprint.

Those who are slapping a carnal building together and "shifting" things by their own design should take heed because they may have just shifted off of the foundation. We do not shift the foundation; the foundation shifts and changes us into becoming His HOUSE. The definition for FOUNDATION is an established sub-structure. It means to set, to appoint, and to get footing. Foundation is something FOUND.

If you have become weary in building and you have lost sight of the passion for doing so in the first place, GO TO THE FOUNDATION. It is time to get on our knees (even lay flat before God) because that is when we are closest to the blueprint. If you are in a particular stage of a relationship where you and your friend, business partner, or perhaps your spouse have hit a rut, and progress together for the future seems impossible, lay down your opinions, your plans, your issues, and revisit the foundation. Drop any self-centered pride that may have disrupted the progress of your protocol. While many have made the word "forgiveness" a super emotional religious thing, it is actually simple corrective protocol that releases us from the weight of guilt so we can get back on track with the King's purpose and development.

We need to also realize that we are being built on an ETERNAL FOUNDATION whose Maker is the Alpha and Omega, Almighty God. The Kingdom Adam lost put our connection with eternal God out of reach, but in DUE TIME, Jesus (the second Adam) reconnected us to activate the FOUNDATION of God's KINGDOM back into the earth. The PROTOCOL of reconciliation, redemption, and restoration re-established God's original plan.   God is continually REDEEMING the TIME to realign us with His ETERNAL plan, giving His people a MANDATE to transform entire nations.

REVIEW OF PRINCIPLES
IN CHAPTER FIVE

1. We cannot progress in this journey as an island all by ourselves.

2. How we interact with people will determine how far we get in the progress of our purpose.

3. Before God constructs great accomplishments through us, He cultivates our character.

4. Vision and Purpose are not in our current stage of building; they are in the foundation.

5. The Foundation of our household brings accountability, integrity, and accuracy.

CHAPTER SIX
THE PROTOCOL OF APPREHENDING
PROGRESS THROUGH DOORS

Apprehending what has apprehended us is literally a series of transitions through "doors" both inside the household of God and out into the world as well. Jesus said: "I am the Door" (John 10:9). He did not just say He had a door; He said that He IS THE DOOR!

We often think of *doors* as opportunities, but *doors* also represent checkpoints, transition, and paradigm change. The Greek word for "door" is "thura," which means portal, opening or closing, and entry examination. We don't just stroll through Kingdom doors with all kinds of baggage. In Matthew 19:24, Jesus told the rich young ruler, "It is easier for a camel to go through the eye of a needle than for a rich man to enter into the kingdom of God." The rich man here is depicted as one who had a lot of baggage (stuff), and was not willing to have it "checked" to enter into new levels of Kingdom life.

Some get annoyed with airport security and the protocols they have to observe to get safely through to their plane. No matter how important we are, everybody MUST take their shoes off and put their bags into a bin to be pushed through a machine. It can be embarrassing especially if a person "beeps" as they go through the doorway and have to be further examined. Many people complain, but for their safety and the safety of others, it is imperative that baggage filled with weapons and questionable devices not go through. The same is true in the Kingdom of God as we pass through to new thresholds. To get through the door, we must drop our pride and then God will promote us through (to new thresholds of Kingdom life).

We cannot move through Kingdom doors with the heavy baggage of the past on our backs. Baggage may include unforgiveness, bitterness, and resentment. Jesus will not allow us to bring heavy garments or fleshly weapons into His Embassy, so He requires that we allow Him to cleanse us daily and follow the protocol that changes us every time we step through the door to another level. These doors are extremely important because the threshold to another level always births a fresh vision. Too many people are sitting in the holding cells of life (wondering why they are not getting anywhere) because they refused to part with their weapons.

I have had the honor of visiting the Knesset in Jerusalem and I found out quickly that you do not just drop in, but you go through the protocol of security clearance, and several doors before even getting to the foyer. Ambassadors from several countries were in attendance. They all had to go through the security check points, they all had to take off their shoes and belts, but never once complained about the protocol necessary to enter in. None of them had an attitude of supremacy or imposition because they were not representing themselves; they were representing their countries. Each of them humbly did whatever was necessary to go through the door. When I went to Nigeria and was invited to attend chapel with the President of that country, I had to go through many detailed checkpoints as I entered the Presidential compound, but I had no difficulty obeying their protocols because they were keeping me safe.

We must be willing to drop "self" to enter into strategic doors of advance. To enter God's presence there is protocol that is not legalistic or ceremonial, but meant for cleansing and examination. Jesus became our access, the DOOR of entry to the Father. When it comes to the Kingdom of God, the outer courts are open for all to come, but the inner court of God's temple has many checkpoints and examinations allowing the process to refine and purify us. This is not about jumping through the religious "hoops" of man-made traditions, but cultivating Kingdom lifestyle through process. It will require that we humble ourselves enough to be purified, and it will also expedite the progress of our promotion. Coming into the door of the holy of holies is a deeply significant entrance. Examination is never condemnation, butpurification for purpose. How we enter His gates and courts will determine how we go forth into nations with His authority and impact. We are Kingdom representatives. Doorway protocol exists in every nation for entry. Ambassadors realize the value of going through doors properly. We never go through Kingdom doors alone (even though we go through individually) because we are interconnected to others that are observing our conduct to measure theirs.

Embassies are always planted on foreign soil. This earth was made foreign through Adam's sin, but God sent His Son to redeem it, and He is now sending His Ambassadors out (in His name) to reconcile what was lost. How we go through doors will determine how much diplomatic immunity we have in hostile lands. Many pray for God to OPEN DOORS of advancement, but they do not fully identify that a door set before them is first a passageway of development. Knowing we have been apprehended by God-ordained purpose and destiny is exciting, but not knowing how to "get through to it" can result in frustration. DOORS represent portals and defining shifts in our lives. A door is literally a BEGINNING entered into. Here are four factors of Kingdom doors:

1. DOORS worry the devil. In 1 Corinthians 16:9, the Apostle Paul said, "For a great door and effectual is opened unto me, and there are many adversaries." An open door is clear indication that we are stepping into an important new season. The devil sends adversaries (who are "adverse" to us going through), seeking to distract us from our true purpose by presenting "short cuts" and counterfeit passageways leading to false promotions that crash and burn.

2. DOORS cultivate us. Every door has a "threshold," and when it comes to God ordained Kingdom doors, this is more than a casual step over into something new. The threshold of His doors shape, mold, and cultivate us into His image. We cannot take an "old" us into a new place, so genuine Kingdom doors will "thresh and hold" us until all the carnal mindsets are purged out. PROGRESS through Kingdom doors means we are PROCESSED first.

3. Doors get us through PLACES. PLACES have entry points and EVERY DOOR has specific protocol (order of proceeding) connected to it. For example, Doors usually represent the inner rooms in a "household," but GATES represent governmental territories and authorities. If we are at a "gate" of authority and treat it like a "door" of opportunity we will find it locked. This is why it is VITAL to discern the purpose of the particular door we are standing in front of.

4. DOORS are RELATIONAL CONNECTORS. These doors unite individual rooms into a FITLY FRAMED HOUSE, CULTIVATING a KINGDOM COMMUNITY. We are not called to be isolated islands, but a CONNECTED **Kingdom household** of saints who know how to interconnect destinies for Kingdom purpose. Helping others find their doors results in discovering ours, and going through our doors helps others go through theirs.The devil tries to get us to shut our doors to one another through hurts, but we as Kingdom citizens have the authority to **shut down the "gates" of hell** when we STAY UNITED as Ambassadorial doors of the King's Embassy!

God **CONNECTIONS** are vital to knowing our doors. Ephesians chapter 4 reveals that God has set **GATES** (offices) of His authority to train and perfect saints into their Kingdom stature as a **FITLY FRAMED** (united community) to manifest the King of kings into the world. The result is that we become **GATES** and **DOORS** (open portals) of Kingdom manifestation into the earth. No matter what is going on in the world's governments or economies, we are citizens of God's household (interconnected doors) resourcing His WEALTH. Psalm 24:9 says: "Lift up your heads oh ye GATES and be ye lifted up ye everlasting DOORS and the KING of GLORY shall COME IN." **We declare OPEN KINGDOM DOORS! Every door has a "threshold" changing us into the new place we are entering. HOW CAN WE KNOW WHAT DOOR WE ARE FACING?** Our first focus is not on the current "door," but on the Lord Who is the Door.

REVIEW OF THE PRINCIPLES
IN CHAPTER 6

1. We often think of doors as opportunity, but doors also represent checkpoints, transition, and change.

2. Doors worry the devil because he knows it means we are progressing to new levels.

3. Doors cultivate us through thresholds that "thresh" and "hold" us until carnal mindsets are purged out.

4. Doors move us into new places of entry.

5. Doors are relational connectors.

6. Gates represent government (or outer borders), but doors represent inner intimacy.

7. It is vital to acknowledge the particular door we are going through in order to conduct ourselves properly.

CHAPTER SEVEN
THE PROTOCOL OF APPREHENDING
THROUGH TRANSITION

It is impossible to go through a door without transitioning to another place. Going through a door means "change," and change involves moving into unfamiliar territory. Most of us know the joy of the wind in our sails as we go forward with propelled success through smooth cooperative waters However, we do not like it when we come to the place of TRANSITION (or crossroads), and we feel there is a shutting down of engines. Trying to push forward in the waters of transition can be frustrating because we seem to have lost our "drive" and are just "going through the motions." Sometimes there is a temptation to PUMP UP what worked yesterday, hoping the engines will kick in and get us out of a "floating" state. Those who try to appear to be going somewhere by repeating the past are going nowhere fast and could end up shipwrecked (1Timothy 1:19).

TRANSITION is part of God's design for character building as it "changes" us before moving us into a place of change. Patience must have a perfection work to be complete and lacking nothing (James 1:4). Some think "patience" is "waiting," but patience is God transitioning our mindsets in the midst of "waiting." A steady sitting ship is healthier than a moving shipwreck going nowhere fast.

Some try to avoid transition because it involves pruning. Pride detests being "cut back" or appearing to be "unsuccessful." As a result, every effort will be made to keep an appearance of "momentum" going, but the boat, while moving, is still only going around in circles in the same spot. Enemies use these times to broadcast your apparent failure to progress forward, but the truth is, TRANSITION is God's way of preventing us from going full steam into a wall. In times of transition people may ask if you are okay, and you may not know how to answer them. You feel like avoiding everybody, and perhaps even moving away to another city to "start over" as your ego takes a beating. We must realize, however, that TRANSITION is not the "end" of the road, but a SHIFT to a new "paradigm" (from where we've been) into the new level (or reference point) of progressive purpose. Transition must take place before transformation can fully manifest.

There is a word that brings with it the functional essence of protocol, and that simple word is COME. Most think the word "come" means to suddenly "be here," but while something may seem to have quickly appeared, it had to process to manifest. Nothing "just happens." Jesus made it clear that God's Kingdom would COME by His will being DONE in earth as it is in heaven (Matthew 6:10). In order for anything of God to COME, it must have the protocol of order.

A great business deal never falls into your lap or "just happens." It was processing through many dimensions of development that you could not see and ultimately culminated into what appeared to have suddenly happened. However, if you are in a business that basically sells gimmicks with no process at the root of its operations, you may want to think about changing companies because success that "pops in" can most certainly "pop out." Always remember that the process of sound protocol is your friend.

We live in a world of instant fixes and microwave results, but what God calls DONE involves a transition to fully COME. When it happens (or manifests) is not when it began. James 5:8 says that the coming of the Lord draws (or processes) near. In the westernized church world, a move of God is often referred to as the sudden appearance of miracles or mass healing in a church service that seem to come out of nowhere, but those outward sudden indicators are not the "move" of God, they are the "manifestation" of God. A MOVE of God is not visible; it is a process of transitioning and developing underground unseen by the physical eye, and once that move is full term, it becomes a manifestation bursting up through the ground of harvest. People often miss the move that provided the deeper message and reason for the manifestation because they get so fixated on one miraculous manifestation. This is why many churches get stuck. They seek to repeat a manifestation without understanding the move (or purpose) of God and become denominations (or a camp) around a single historical event. God never has to repeat what He did.

God is constantly transitioning us into where He wants us to go in order to fulfill His purpose. When we use the phrase "move of God" we must understand that God does not move anywhere because He is already there. God is MOVING us into where He already is. The great revivals of church history were really meant to be transitional reference points of God moving us into greater dimensions of His Kingdom restoration. The most frustrated people are those whose season has changed, but their mind never got the memo. Sometimes God allows us to feel uneasy and desperate for change so we will wake up to the fact we have already progressed to new levels. We need to allow the transitional protocols to move us up to those new levels.

They that wait (serve and set purpose) upon the Lord shall renew(shift, transition) their strength (ability, clarity, understanding). They shall mount up (rise to new level, shift paradigms) WITH WINGS (extended launch, direction) AS EAGLES (sharp sighted, purposed). THEY SHALL RUN (with vision) AND NOT BE WEARY, WALK (lifestyle courage) AND NOT FAINT (See Isaiah 40:31) God is pruning away the old feathers so we can RISE with greater WINGS. I admonish you not to despise TRANSITION, but instead, EMBRACE IT!

A Review of the Principles in Chapter Seven

1. Transition is part of God's design for character building.

2. To COME is a transitional word that indicates something is drawing near or processing.

3. A "move" of God takes place underground, and when it fully develops, it will manifest for all to see.

4. Waiting on the Lord is a process of renewing our strength to mount up higher.

CHAPTER EIGHT
THE PROTOCOL OF
APPREHENDING THE KEYS

We have referred to KEYS as principles, and while that is true, we need to go deeper to understand the greater definition. KEYS are literally Kingdom passports and visas backed with governmental authority to open and close doors and give God's people entry. Keys are uniquely shaped for specific DOORS. Kingdom keys will not fit religious doors or man made motives. The reason Jesus said, "I give unto you the keys of the Kingdom" is because He is the key to the Kingdom. (See Matthew 16:19.) These KEYS take us to NEW LEVELS and ports of entry. Jesus established His church upon a ROCK of revelation and then gave us KEYS.

The church is defined as the "ekklesia," the called out ones. We have been called out of darkness and translated into the Kingdom of God's Son. We are in this world, but not of this world. The world (in scripture) is not referring to the physical "earth." The definition for "world" is "cosmos" or "an order (system/ cycle) of a government." We have been called out of the corruption of the world's system and translated into God's Kingdom authority. (See 1 Peter 2:9; Colossians 1:13.)

As God's ambassadors (representatives) in the world through His church (Kingdom Embassy) we have been given diplomatic immunity. Only Kingdom citizens can use Kingdom keys because we are representing the authority of the King. This is why Jesus said, "I will BUILD (process, set in order, and fitly frame) My church (a global Kingdom embassy) and the gates of hell (or enemy strongholds) shall not prevail against it" (Matthew 16:18). We are subject to the King's plan; we don't just arbitrarily use the keys to get in wherever we want. As representatives of the King, we should never abuse our privilege of walking in His authority in order to build our own empires or agendas. These keys of the Kingdom OPEN gates and doors between heaven and earth to accomplish the manifestation of His Kingdom. That is why Jesus prayed, "Thy Kingdom come, Thy will be done, ON earth as it is IN heaven" (Matthew 6:10). We have been given access into governments, economies, and nations.

When we think of "keys" we think of "doors." It is also interesting to notice that our computers have keyboards, and it is the combination (or protocol) of typed letters that opens our screens producing a release of information. Pianos have "keys" that, when played in a protocol of chord progressions, produce beautiful music. When a key goes into a door it becomes the agent of protocol that activates the tumblers to advance. The key goes through the door before we do. This key is the living Word of God in our mouths, and is PROPHETIC piercing through to where we are headed. When we prophesy to our Kingdom destiny (declaring the King's Word), we are inserting His KEY into the mechanism that opens heaven and closes hell. God is opening the NATIONS to the GOOD NEWS of Jesus Christ and His Kingdom, but He is using Ambassadors who know how to use their KEYS.

Too many believers are sitting at prophetic doors of destiny and are not going through simply because they do not know what they have in their hands. The KEYS of the KINGDOM are passports and visas into new dimensions and perimeters of spreading the Gospel. When customs agents see your passport they are not seeing you, they are seeing the entire government of the country you are representing. That passport is your KEY into places you could not go without it.

The Body of Christ has talked for years about God's Kingdom as it relates to heaven, referring to it as a place we are going to when we die. Death, however, is not the port of entry into God's Kingdom. Life in Jesus is the door of entry, and we have the KEYS of the Kingdom now to use for entry into every phase of our purpose and destiny. This passport gives you the entire Kingdom backing you need to advance through DOORS of progress. We are in a day when we are going beyond passports into VISAS that open governments, economies, and nations to us as agents of change with Kingdom authority. Visas allow more involvement of transactions and interaction within nations.

A few years ago I stood at a hotel door and stared at a card they had given me. I wondered why they gave me a "card" instead of a "key." Embarrassed, I went back to the front desk and told the lady she gave me a "card" instead of a room key. She responded: "Mr. Kendall, that card IS your room key." I was astounded because I had not seen anything like that before. Sure enough, I slid the card into the door slot and a green light beamed indicating I could open the door. My initial problem was not the keycard; it was not knowing how to make it work. My concepts were too outdated for a progressive new protocol. We can stand at the doors of destiny lamenting the good old days, or we can just open the door with the Kingdom keys God has put in our hands, realizing we have come to new levels that require afresh revelation of God's port of entry. What's that you have in your hand? A Kingdom passport, and it is stamped with an open VISA. Let's use it!

Review of Principles
in Chapter 8

1. Keys are passports and visas given by God to open doors.

2. We have been given access into governments, economies, and nations to accomplish God's purpose.

3. The key goes through the door before we do.

4. Passports and visas give us the full backing of the country we represent.

Chapter Nine
The Protocol of
Apprehending in PLACES

The "pro-to-our-call" that has apprehended us is not really about us. It is a call to something beyond us; it involves a quest to restore God's Kingdom. Isaiah 58:12 says: "And they that shall be of thee shall build old waste places (compare to Isaiah 61:4); you shall raise up the foundations of many generations and be called, The repairer of the breach, the restorers of paths to dwell in." What places were lost? Adam lost the Kingdom.

The second Adam, Jesus, restored communion between God and man, thus activating recovery and reconnection of the King's dominion on earth through His regenerated people. Now the devil and the principalities of darkness war against the Kingdom of Light seeking to blind people from the truth and infect mankind with deeper corruption in a last ditch attempt to derail God's plan. However, Satan is already defeated and Kingdom citizens are multiplying to reclaim ground. Before we can "take places" we must "take our place" by understanding our authority and position.

Our PLACE is established, not in current issues, but in prophetic destiny and that destiny is activated NOW. God set our PLACE, and then made us to sit in heavenly PLACES (positions) of authority far above all principalities and powers. (See Ephesians 1:3; 1:20; 2:6; 3:10.)Each one of us has a distinct purpose and ordained call of God on our lives, and the process of protocol will flow through the measure of that call. This is important to understand because in order to infiltrate into "places" we must know our "place." Operating within our measure and mantle will allow us to hear God's strategy (protocol of maneuvers) through places to change entire paradigms. We are in the world and not of it, but the cultivation of the Kingdom of God involves infiltration and influence of wisdom to get into nations first diplomatically rather than by an adversarial approach. This is not about compromise; it is about relevance to impact the world. In order to effectively take our "place" we must understand the particular function of specific "places" so that we know how to conduct ourselves. Examples of these atmospheres and places are as follows:

1. **Realms: dimensions of rule**
2. **Borders: distinction of boundaries**
3. **Spheres: definitions of influence**
4. **Territories: districts of government**
5. **Gates: of government/ cities/nations (outer entry)**
6. **Doors: in a house/ room/ intimacy (inner entry)**
7. **Windows: open perception and ability to see outside of our current location**

God never intended for us to "walk" through windows and "look" through doors. In fact, Jesus made it clear that those who avoid the door and try to come in through a "window" are identified as thieves and robbers. (See John 10:1.) Some Christians will talk of 10/40 windows to go through. They probably mean that "windows" are "moments" to seize something, but protocol makes it clear we do not "seize" through windows, we "SEE" (vision) through windows what can be obtained through the PROCESS of the DOOR. The same is often true with those trying to slam through a wall and calling it "breakthrough" when true breakthrough is simply opening the right DOOR. We must know the difference between the personal passage of a DOOR and the governmental GATE of a city or authority. We cannot run into these atmospheres and just start sermonizing. There is a protocol of behavior we need to follow in each one of these places to effectively pull down principalities and strongholds. The realms, borders, spheres, territories, gates, and doors must be renovated and restored back to the dominion of our King and His Kingdom. God will get us into places if He knows we will not abuse our authority and rip places apart for our own self-promotion.

REVIEW OF PRINCIPLES IN CHAPTER 9

1. The "places laid wasted" refers to the Kingdom, lost by Adam's fall, but restored by Jesus.

2. Our place is not established in current issues, but by prophetic destiny already set.

3. In order to effectively take places, we must take our place.

4. The main dimensions of places are set as realms, borders, spheres, territories, gates, doors, and windows.

CHAPTER TEN
THE PROTOCOL OF APPREHENDING
THROUGH ADVERSITY

Some may be reading this book and thinking, "This protocol stuff would be great if we operated in a perfect world where there was never a crisis or a problem." The truth is: Kingdom protocol will actually turn crisis into innovation and problems into potential for greater progress. One of the proving factors in the confirmation process of your God-ordained purpose is CHALLENGE. The 3 specific challenges are ***opposition, adversaries, and obstacles.***

Men and women responding to God's call into ministry have confirmation services where elder ministers publically acknowledge and officially endorse them as credible and set for activated service. While this is scriptural and while this is a vital public seal by elders (as listed in 1 Timothy 4:14), it must be understood that this is not the full CONFIRMATION process. This process actually starts with a personal revelation and covenant between you and God to become all that He says you already are. The activation of that confirmation is usually jump-started with a challenge.

Whether or not the commission is to an office within the church or out in the marketplace, we have all been ORDAINED of God to specific PURPOSE. We need to know, however, that even though God has ordained us, that does not mean that we will automatically fulfill our purpose. As we discussed in prior chapters, PURPOSE is birthed first out of WHO and WHY we are before it is expressed in producing WHAT we do (or produce). CONFIRMATION must be a process of personal discovery and development more than just a ceremonial accomplishment or obtained title. In order to TRANSFORM into the character and stature of God's purposed design, there must be another piece to the process of confirmation. That piece is the ability to overcome challenges.

In Jeremiah 1:5-10, God told Jeremiah that before He was formed He knew him, sanctified him, and ORDAINED him a prophet unto the nations. In order for this ORDINATION to be CONFIRMED, Jeremiah would have to OVERCOME the opposing faces of threatening people to root out, pull down, destroy, and throw down the challenges as one who had been SET over the nations to build and plant. Throughout the Bible we read that when oppositions arose, it was a clear indication that God's ORDAINED plan was being birthed (breaking through to new ground). Hebrews 6:16-19 makes it clear that God's confirmation ends all strife, giving us an anchor of HOPE to lay hold of. If in what we are doing, we continue to struggle to make it happen through our own carnal determination, we may be working our own plan "for God" instead of allowing God's plan to work IN us. If in the midst of challenge, we can rest in the Lord and allow Him to move through us, we will overcome all obstacles.

The three challenges that actually help to confirm our ordained purpose are:

1. **Opposition: to distract** us when we receive a revelation and vision.

2. **Adversaries: to detain us** when we are at the open door of a new season.

3. **Obstacles: to deceive us** when we think there is no way to get through.

Defeating these challenges is not about being "battle" minded. The enemy brings opposition, adversaries, and obstacles because he is nervous about the progress we are making.

We should not be alarmed in these times of difficulty. We should see these challenges as the greatest confirmations of our God ordained VICTORY. When it seems impossible, our God-given PURPOSE will break forth into innovations, ideas, and a Kingdom economy that overcomes the world. (See I John 5:4.) In too many cases we have become too "combat-minded" instead of "advance-minded." While the warfare of kingdoms against the Kingdom rage on (and the attacks are real), we must never go on the warpath of "reaction" causing us to lose our path of progress. If the devil thinks he can get away with it, he will try to keep us stomping out fires he continually sets just to keep us from advancing into our greater purpose. The battle is the Lord's and He has called us to OVERCOME the world with the advantage of infrared FAITH that sees beyond the enemies and on into victory. When God's Word speaks of us being GOOD SOLDIERS (in 2 Timothy 2:4), it is not using the term "soldier" as a "buck private" in the Army. The Greek word for soldier is "stratologeo" (or literally a STRATEGIST). We may be moving physically from a terrestrial place, but our wisdom comes from above stratospheric (strategy) levels and heavenly places where our perspectives are set. (See Ephesians 2:6.)

We are not planning battle maneuvers from the bunker or foxholes, but from the General's tent. It is there that God prepares a table of ideas, innovations, and strategy for us even in the presence of our enemies. 2 Timothy 2:4 goes on to say that no man in warfare gets himself entangled with the affairs of the current situation because Kingdom strategy looks past the crisis into the prophetic outcome, and is never focused on the current conflict. We have been given the General's focus, which is always on the CONQUEST.

Review of Principles
in Chapter 10

1. Kingdom protocol will actually turn a crisis into an innovation.

2. Three challenges that confirm our ordained purpose are opposition, adversaries, and obstacles.

3. Confirmation is the process of discovery and development beyond ceremonies and titles.

4. We are strategists that look beyond the conflict into the conquest.

CHAPTER ELEVEN
THE PROTOCOL OF
APPREHENDING CHARACTER

It becomes clear after grasping the complexity of our Kingdom mandate that we as saints are changing, developing, and growing through this entire process. Jumping into levels of challenge before we are ready can sideline us and bring needless pressure. For this reason, God sets the shaping of our character as a priority even above our successful deeds. While protocol is moving us through to the fulfillment of purpose, it is also revealing our purpose through every phase of discovery in who we are. To skip submission to authority, training, and obedience to discipline will only violate the protocol that gets us where we need to go. A disciple is a follower of a teaching, but must go on to become a protégé (one who becomes the teaching), and then goes on to find their own voice. Protégé comes from the word "protect" and signifies someone submitted to **elder guidance** for launching of their own purpose and career. The developmental protocol of mentoring reveals:

a.   CALLING: distinct purpose from inside
b.   APPOINTMENT: as ordained, established, and positioned
c.   ASSIGNMENT: committed, charged, and set forth

It is with the degree that we will humble ourselves to be cultivated by God's process that we will rise into our greatest potential. With all the power at His disposal, Jesus Himself was tutored before He taught, bringing the example of total submission to His Father who sent him. Too often a novice emerges because either there was no submission to an elder authority or because there was no nurturing elder willing to mentor. There are too many spiritual babies trying to be spiritual fathers before their time. For some the process of growth and maturity is quenched due to those presumed to be "spiritual fathers" who are really only seeking perpetual followers through control or subservience. Stalling the protocol and development of someone's purpose is an exposure of carnal fear and ignorance to the culture of God's Kingdom.

The truth is, bringing up sons and daughters that excel you actually multiplies your impact on the world for God's glory. Passing the torch never means your light goes out, but it actually causes it to burn brighter as it shifts the transitioning elder into greater levels of service than they could ever imagine. Raising spiritual sons and daughters is not about implanting our own ministry DNA or "branding" our name on an upcoming champion. The apostle Paul revealed clear protocol procedure when he said that he was a type of surrogate representation of the Father, "till Christ be formed fully in a protégé." (See Galatians 4:19.)A son (or daughter) will learn from the surrogate parent and even copy them until they discover who they are, and then from a spiritual perspective, they will grow into the DNA of God and His distinct purpose in their lives. The goal is not to make a copy of a copy, but to birth originals. There are four basic stages of maturity development:

1. SHEEP LEVEL: Following stage where they need the MILK (Matthew 10)

2. SERVANT LEVEL: Training stage (Matthew 28:20)

3. SON LEVEL: Guidance stage beginning to process MEAT (Galatians 4:1,2)

4. SAINTS LEVEL: Empowering and releasing stage (Romans 8:19)

All these stages are vital to the producing of character and integrity because talent and charisma alone will not stand under heavy storms. The aspect we need to remember about God's classroom is that most of it is "on the job training." Sitting in physical classrooms (and in church services) hearing instruction is important, but it is only in application to daily life that protocol can move us along into new levels of growth.

There are two main fears we need to overcome so protocol can function without interruption. The first is the **FEAR of FAILURE.** It is not that we try to fail, but in seeking to be what God says we are, there will be times when we miss it. Character is not shaped when we are knocked down, but when we get back up wiser. The biggest obstacle to overcome in failure is not the failure, but the carnal pride that hates to look bad in front of people. Jesus referred to Himself as the Vine and defined us as His branches. Many people imagine a wonderful scene of a glowing tree with beautiful foliage sprouting forth happily ever after, but Jesus goes on to describe how healthy growth will continue; it is by CUTTING BACK (or pruning) the branches stripping them of leaves and all that former glorious fruit. Why? So they can once again remember that their purpose and source is in the Vine and not in their accomplishment. The result of this pruning is even more fruit through the branch as true representatives of the Vine. Focusing on the fruit we produced yesterday will only result in a moldy and wrinkled presentation of the past.

The second is the **FEAR of SUCCESS.** Some may think: "How could anyone be afraid of success?" The fear may not be in the initial success, but in maintaining it. If we think "success" is about accomplishments and achievements then we will be jumping through "hoops" the rest of our lives instead of growing through the genuine protocol of lasting advance. The dictionary defines success as the result, outcome, or gaining of fame, but the biblical definition of success is more than an accomplishment; it is literally a "succession" (or process) and ultimate advance of many connected developments. In other words, success may actually have many failures in it, but not repeating mistakes fuels advance with the protocol of wisdom. We need not fear maintaining "success" because true success is not about maintaining; it is about gaining a series of steps that move us into a larger goal. This is why the apostle Paul declares: "This one thing I do, I forget what's behind by reaching forward to the things ahead to apprehend what has apprehended me" (Philippians 3:13).

As the protocol of character building progresses and cultivates who we are, there is less of the "us" we thought we were, but more of who we really are and who God is in us. This is why Jesus said that those who will lay down a false image of who they think they are will discover who they really are through Me (Matthew 10:39). We must understand that as Kingdom protocol progresses in us we will transition and change on a daily basis into becoming who we really are. Sometimes it is hard to identity what we are becoming, but the priority is to keep looking to the Author and Refiner of our development as we change from glorious revelation to glorious discovery. We can't afford to find a comfortable place to stop processing, because if we do, we will be a caricature of what we could have been instead of building the complete character of what we are becoming.

REVIEW OF PRINCIPLES
IN CHAPTER 11

1. We are called, appointed, and assigned, but first we must submit to training.

2. It is to the degree that we humble ourselves to be cultivated by God's process that we will rise to our potential.

3. The four levels of character development are sheep, servants, sons, and saints.

4. We must develop courage that overcomes the fear of failure as well as the fear of success.

CHAPTER TWELVE
PROTOCOL OF APPREHENDING OUR LEADERSHIP ROLES

In the quest of apprehending our purpose, we will find that while we continue to be students, at some point we are becoming teachers (and leaders). All of these developments we have shared in the prior chapters will bring us to a stature of leadership whether it is influencing entire nations or effectively impacting the lives of friends. There are various levels of leadership and particular protocols according to function of authority, but here we will deal with leadership in general. Some of you reading this might say you have no desire to lead anybody, but God's purpose in you will impact people and challenge their paradigms. You will become a standard bearer that they watch to begin grasping their purpose.

The word "leader" is only used six times in the Bible (and only once in the New Testament). It is interchangeable with words like officer, governor, commander, captain, ruler, teacher, and example. Here are two aspects of God-ordained leaders:

1. A leader is a visionary who ignites people into grasping their destiny as leaders.
2. True leaders don't seek permanent followers, but attract leaders in training who follow.

A leader must be going somewhere in order to lead people in getting there. There must be a coupling of visionary and leader because a visionary may see great things, but it takes leadership to transition people into manifesting vision. A leader leads by prophetic vision into places they have been before they arrive, and then they transition people to get there. Jesus said, "The things that I do, you will do also and greater works than these shall you do because I go to My Father" (John 14:12). If a leader does not birth a leader that excels him, that leader is just babysitting. A visionary with no leadership is only a dreamer without a mandate. It is amazing to see the process and restoration of Kingdom leadership throughout the Bible:

a. **The Old Testament:** Purpose lost but not destroyed/ Vision prophesied.

b. **The Gospels**: THE VISION manifested of the King and Kingdom

c. **The Book of Acts:** Activation of **MISSION (on the job training)**

d. **The Epistles to the churches** (corporate cultivation and training):

Romans: Entrance into light and change of lifestyle 1 & 2 Corinthians: Personal: Motives= Mindset= Manner

Galatians: Developing the understanding of freedom

Ephesians: Equipping saints into a stature and stand

Philippians: Exercising tenacity to PRESS into the PRIZE

Colossians: Becoming visionaries with examination of motivations.

1 & 2 Thessalonians: Expectation based on the

foundation

e. **The Epistles to young visionaries**:
1 & 2 Timothy: Qualifications and order to fight the good fight
Titus: Character and integrity essentials
Philemon: Restoration to potential

f. **The Book of Hebrews:** The transitional process from the Old Covenant to the New Covenant.

g. **The Guides to Sustained Leadership** are outlined in:
James: Our MIND and our MOUTH
1 & 2 Peter: Our WALK and our RELATIONSHIPS
1, 2, & 3 John: Our LOVE and its TESTS
Jude: Discernment and Examination

h. **The Book of Revelation:** Culmination of an eternal restoration as kings and priests.

It is so exciting to see the succession, progression, and restoration of God's authority to man and the recovery of the dominion once lost through Adam's fall. Kingdom leadership is crucial to helping people understand the course they are on. The focus of leaders is not to get people to accomplish the purpose and vision of the leader, but to ignite purpose and vision in people to cultivate God's Kingdom here on earth as it is in heaven. As leaders in corporate vision we have often thought people should "catch" our vision; however, there are no second hand visions. People can carry out a corporate mission through a leader's vision, but in order for a community to become a united team, a corporate vision must ignite unique individual and creative visions in each person to reveal how they fit united in a corporate plan.

This moves vision from micro-management with followers into team empowerment. Community protocol cannot just move through the leader and then stop at a limp core of people. A visionary leader will become the chief igniter of the visions interconnecting each specific participant. Pastors who focus on expecting followers to "catch their vision" will see people excited for about five years, but then the excitement grows thin as people begin to wonder if they might have a vision too. If there is no place for them to expand their vision, or incorporate it into the bigger picture, they leave. If a corporate vision is about training people to grasp their God-given purpose and vision, that church or business will not lose people, but will actually send them out, constantly multiplying new protégés.

The protocol of leadership has not been allowed to function fully in many churches, and Therefore, we have generated too many empires and subcultures instead of manifested Kingdom embassies. This is changing as God is raising up leaders with sons and daughters who excel their mentors and multiply ambassadors all over the world.

REVIEW OF PRINCIPLES
IN CHAPTER 12

1. A leader is a visionary who ignites people to grasp their destiny as leaders.

2. True leaders do not seek permanent followers. True leaders attract leaders in training who follow.

3. A leader must be going somewhere in order to lead people in getting there.

4. If a leader does not birth a leader that excels him, that leader is just babysitting.

CHAPTER THIRTEEN
THE PROTOCOL OF APPREHENDING SOUND ECONOMY

As protocol advances us through many layers of obtaining the fulfillment of purpose, there is one aspect of protocol that is so very vital but often overlooked that it causes many to fall short of apprehending their potential (and even causing others to make shipwreck). That element is the protocol of economy. When we say "economy" most will instantly think of "money," and therein lies part of the problem. Ephesians 2:19 says we are fellow-citizens of God's household. The word "household" comes from the Greek word "okonomia," which means economy. Economy is the management, administration, and dispensation of the King's resources.

We are in a time when "isms" such as socialism, communism, and even capitalism are all being shaken more than ever before, and some nervously wonder what they will do if these economies collapse. There is another ECONOMY, not set in any of those systems, kept hidden from the religious and the world's systems; it is called Kingdom economy. The greatest hindrance to grasping God's economy is dependence on conventional world thinking. While there are pieces of biblical principles in the economic "isms" of the world, they actually operate backwards from the protocol God set forth. The world's economy is based in debt that pays for yesterday today, but Kingdom wealth is set for tomorrow today. The world says, "To have you've got to get," but God's economy declares, "We have because we give." The world's economic philosophy is from the outside in, but the King's economy is from the inside out. God has called us to be stewards of His mysteries, treasures, and resources. It could be said that in order to even begin to be a good steward there must be an understanding of protocol because administration of resources is all about processing resources accurately.

The World's economic system…
Money is **wealth** bringing **riches** to have **treasure.**

Kingdom economics starts with reserves of…
Treasure within us bringing **riches** of strength
that produces **wealth** of ideas drawing a currency of
money.

There are four basic terms used globally but often in very loose and vague terms.

These four terms are:

1. **Treasure**
2. **Riches**
3. **Wealth**
4. **Money**

In the world's economy, "money" is wealth, and the world thinks money gets them riches. Therefore, men and women in that system worship money because it appears to give them worth and value. Corrupted mindsets operate from the logic that without money they have nothing, but with money they can have it all. This brings the backward (debt ridden) philosophy that says that **money** is **wealth** that makes us **rich,** and loading us with **treasure** (or hoarded stuff). Pride and greed are the result. Sad to say, however, the religious-minded have often misquoted the Bible, saying that "money is the root of all evil." However, that is a misrepresentation because it leaves out one simple word can pervert the true meaning. 1 Timothy 6:10 actually says that it is the **"love of money that is the root of all evil."** In other words, it is loving money as though it is wealth that gives place to the evil tactics of the devil whose plan is to blind us to the true treasure.

Money is not wealth; it is only "currency" (a current) set by governments for the exchange of wealth. In fact, American money (as of this writing) still has "IN GOD WE TRUST" as the source of wealth, but unfortunately there are some people and groups trying to remove those words.

The world's perverted protocol binds men and women into a debt mentality that says, "I don't have anything, so if I go work for that guy, he will give some of his money to me and then I'll have it and be worth something." The truth is that you and I are are full of untapped treasure and wealth within, and when someone hires you for a job they are actually bringing you on because they see the treasure in you, and they know you will enrich and prosper their company. That is why they offer currency to transfer your wealth. Often greedy employers pay far too little hoping you will not discover what you are really worth. This is not about getting an inflated ego because we know that everything we have and everything we are is the result of being citizens of God's royal Kingdom. This is one reason why in the world's system some businesses will actually refuse to hire because someone is defined as being too "overqualified."

It is amazing how some marketing schemes will try to convince potential salespeople that if they will promote their product, the product will make them successful practically overnight, and then they proceed to show them pictures of expensive cars and homes they will possess if they just sell that product. The truth is that no product can "make you" anything or give you worth. If you are successful it is because you were successful and prosperous long before that company and product ever found you. It is not what we do that gives us worth, but who we are in the purpose God sets. God gives us power (authority) to GET (release) wealth within us to establish His covenant and purpose (Deuteronomy 8:18). If we do not work our inner wealth we will not eat (or participate in the exchange of currency that would have been attracted to the wealth that should have been displayed through us).

While working a job or business builds character and produces satisfying results, it never makes us wealthy. Joshua 1:8 says that it is not the place that prospers us, but we PROSPER the places as we meditate on God's inward treasure of wisdom and understanding, producing who we are.

Kingdom economics (or KINGDONOMICS) shifts the paradigm back into place as the four major economic indicators (TREASURE, RICHES, WEALTH, and MONEY) are set back in order. God never starts with money (or mammon). He begins with the TREASURE in our earthen vessels (2 Corinthians 4:7), the "reserves" of resources such as knowledge and wisdom. God's economy starts with His SEED of purpose deposited in His creation causing us to become SEED producers. Seed is not money first, but ideas and plans that form through the belly of purpose. Treasure is not "stuff," but reserves where innovations are cultivated. It is these reserved treasures of God in us that bring us RICHES (or strength and supply) to operate. RICHES are really the EARNEST (down-payment) that nourishes us in the process of development. Then when the time comes for some of the enriched reserves to be released, it becomes WEALTH to be brought forth.

Wealth is not fully defined until it is transferred into manifestation and tangible value producing something through us. A current (currency, money) is then drawn to wealth as it is freely given through God's people. Money then is a servant and not the master. This "current" is not drawn just to pay debts or bills. Instead it is drawn to wealthy ideas birthed through God's purpose that will also pay the bills.

God's economy has been hidden from the world's system to be revealed to those who are yielded to His protocol of purpose. He promises to those who listen diligently to the voice of the King and His protocol process, that all these blessings shall come on them and overtake them. This brings the result of a NEW PARADIGM where we become lenders and not borrowers, the head and not the tail, above and not in bondage beneath (along with many other benefits listed in (Deuteronomy 28:1-13).

REVIEW OF PRINCIPLES
IN CHAPTER 13

1. Household comes from the word "okonomia," which means economy.

2. Economy is not just money, but management, administration, and dispensation of the King's resources.

3. In a world where "isms" are shaking, there is another economy that is eternal.

4. Places don't prosper us; we prosper places.

5. God's Kingdom economy operates from the inside out.

6. God's intent is that we be the lenders and not the borrowers, the head and not the tail.

CHAPTER FOURTEEN
THE PROTOCOL OF HONOR AND PROMOTION

It's amazing how perverted and twisted the world has become as "money" is falsely defined as "wealth" bringing further false definitions to words like honor and promotion. Current counterfeit role models declare that fame brings them honor and promotion. These things are so backwards to the truth. Proverbs 15:33 says; "The fear of the Lord is the instruction of wisdom and before honor is humility." This scripture again reveals valuable God ordained protocol that must be processed to make sure our progress is sure. The Dictionary defines "honor" as to esteem, value, and to prize, but inward honor is cultivated through righteousness and integrity. People in today's society loosely use the word "honor" to thank others for recognizing them in an accomplishment, but honor is first about who we are before extolling what we do.

There is no honor among men if they do not honor God. To honor God is more than ceremonial recognition, but it is to allow Him to be Lord and King in every dimension of our lives. In Matthew 15:8 it is recoded that Jesus said; "This people draw nigh unto Me with their mouth, and honor Me with their lips; but their heart is far from Me." Honoring God involves total trust, yieldedness and obedience to Him in order to process the development of our purpose.

It would be one thing if honoring God was just about how we interact with Him, but the greatest tests to proving our degree of honoring God has to do with how we walk this journey with people. There is relational protocol specified in various arenas such as how children should honor their parents, and how adults should never rebuke an elder. Is this because all people representing dads, moms, and elders are worthy of honor in their actions? No, it is because the God ordained position they hold are reference points of our growth. In fact Ephesians 6:2 says that when children honor their father and mother, it carries promise that they will live long on the earth. In the relational protocol between a husband and wife they submit to one another, (not because everything is perfect in their marriage), but they do it as unto the Lord. The relational protocol of honor is difficult when the person is harsh, but God honors those who honor His protocol and even the most difficult relationships can bring growth.

The protocol of authority functions in personal relationships, but becomes a defining factor when it is expressed through offices and governing officials. Honor is set in a standard (the Word) before it is activated in people. People who crave authority before they've submitted to authority seek empty honor. Honoring God ordained offices and His law of life keeps us from dishonor. 1 Peter 2:17 17 says; "Honor all men. Love the brotherhood. Fear God. Honor the king" (or literally those in authority). This is not about becoming slaves to the domination of men, but this is about honoring God's process of protocol that promotes us into our purpose.

True leaders are never dictators seeking followers, but they are equippers of champions. If there is a corrupted person in a legitimate office of authority, then God will give wisdom on how to remove yourself from ungodly abusers, but to do it without bringing dishonor to the office. There are honorable ways to bring opinions, disagreements, and concerns to those in an office of authority, but to disregard an office of legitimate authority is to dishonor God. He knows how to raise one up and bring an ungodly one down if His office is being mishandled.

Many times it is not the person in office who is corrupted, but it is the people who don't like how the official is leading them and they prove this by spreading discord and disunity in the disguise of seeking justice. The Apostle Paul addresses this in James 3:10 when he says; "...My brethren, these things ought not so to be." There is much more that could be said in this regard, but time does not allow more discussion in this book. The key in knowing the protocol of dealing with others is found in Philippians 2:3 that says; "Let nothing be done through strife or vainglory; but in lowliness of mind let each esteem other better than themselves."

Submission, obedience, and esteeming bring us to promotion. Promotion comes to a vessel of honor and develops the vessel to a place of honor in the Lord. It's not what we do that gives us worth, but it's who we are (through cultivating process) that reveals our worth. Honor presets us in a path of cultivated wisdom. Even the word; "promotion" is clearly pro-motion indicating a direction, but premature power results in dishonor and disaster.

Honor is in us now, but needing cultivation through the protocol of wisdom. Honor never focuses on where we are right now, but sets it's reference point into who we are becoming, because that is who God says we have always been even before we were born. In the account of the birth of Christ, the "wise" men did not seek "a baby" but they sought a King. They looked beyond the current eyesight, and had the vision to honor a King. This is proven as they did not bring toys, but they brought gold, frankincense and myrrh to a King declaring the prophetic dimension of honor. Where ever you are in this journey of protocol, don't dishonor your future by allowing your current place to define you, but continue presenting yourself to God with excellence that defines you by your promised future.

REVIEW OF PRINCIPLES
IN CHAPTER 14

1. There is no honor among men if they do not honor God.

2. God honors those who honor His protocol and even the most difficult relationships bring growth.

3. Honor is set in a standard (the Word) before it is activated in people.

4. It's not what we do that gives us worth, but it's who we are (through cultivating process) that reveals our worth.

5. Honor is in us now, but needing cultivation through the protocol of wisdom

SUMMARY
THE PRIMARY PROTOCOL FOR APPREHENDING KINGDOM PURPOSE

This book really has no end in that it is a perpetual yet progressive journey into God's Kingdom cultivation in our lives. God sets the end that ignites our beginning. Jesus said, "Seek first the kingdom of God and His righteousness, and all these things shall be added to you."(Matthew 6:33) FIRST means the primary, number one, and principle focus above all else. The word "principle" means primary, beginning, a ruling factor, and headship or chief. This refers to the point of origin and is associated with the Greek word "logos" or "first thought." A principal thing can become a principality or rule.

When we seek first God's Kingdom we will discover PURPOSE, and then His righteousness develops the PERSON God has imaged within us, and then all these things (or PERSPECTIVES) will be added to give us navigation through each stage of development. Seeking first the kingdom is literally seeking first the King. Not just seeking Him for His "things," but seeking Him for Who He is, and worshipping Him as Lord over every aspect of our lives. Seeking FIRST the King gives us the King's vision. Seeking FIRST the Kingdom is primary protocol, as it is above all preparation before performance.

When the Apostle Paul spoke of apprehending what had apprehended him, he was not talking about an emotion (even though it no doubt made him feel very emotional), and he was not just talking about a current event or excitement over an accomplishment. Paul was describing a connection with eternal purpose that had ignited his very reason for being. His response was to be totally yielded to press, process, and follow the protocol it would take to advance toward the prize of that high call of God in Christ Jesus.

The time of God allowing shortcuts and lukewarm apathy is over, as only those who will seek first the Kingdom and His protocol for cultivation of His purpose will arrive to hear Him say, "Well done good and faithful servant, enter in" (Matthew 25:21, 23). Until that time, there is a whole lot of living to enjoy and progress to participate in.

What will you do with this fire within you that has apprehended you? You can see that God has not left your future to chance, but has provided all the protocol, process, and protection you need to activate your journey. Whether you are just starting, or in the middle of this cultivating process, may I challenge you to keep moving forward; don't look back because the best is yet to come. God richly bless you. I'll see you on the road as we get there together.

EMBASSY
PUBLISHING

Do you need a speaker?

Do you want Dr. Rick Kendall to speak to your group or event? Then email Dr. Rick Kendall at:
drrickkendall@outlook.com

Whether you want to purchase bulk copies of *Apprehended* or buy another book for a friend, you can contact us at:
embassypublish@aol.com or call (817) 213-7767

If you have a book that you would like to publish, you may contact Embassy Publishing at (817) 213-7767 or email: embassypublish@aol.com